GOING ON A DIG

GOING ON A DIG

Velma
Ford
Morrison

Illustrated with
photographs

DODD, MEAD &
COMPANY
New York

ILLUSTRATIONS COURTESY OF:

D. R. Baston, 14, 24, 36, 44 *bottom,* 47, 50, 51, 52, 54, 55, 56, 57, 60, 62 *top,* 64, 65, 66, 69, 70 *bottom,* 71, 73 *bottom,* 75, 85; Foundation for Illinois Archaeology, 12, 21, 37, 49, 53, 59, 61, 62 *bottom,* 67, 68, 76, 81, 83; Foundation for Illinois Archaeology, Photo by D. R. Baston, 117; Dr. Harold Hutchinson, *title page,* 58, 70 *top,* 72, 86; Illinois State Museum, 15, 22, 29, 39, 43, 46; Illinois State Museum, by permission of Illinois Archaeological Survey, 93; Illinois State Museum, Photo by Marlin Roos, 44 *top,* 112 *top;* Illinois State Museum, by permission of Site Superintendent, Cahokia Mounds State Park, 90, 91; Iowa State Archaeology Department, 42, 114; William C. Morey, *Ancient Peoples,* American Book Company, 27, 32, 35; Hugh Morrison, 18, 73 *top,* 74; Museum of New Mexico, Photo by George C. Bennett, 109; National Park Service, 88 *bottom;* Ohio Historical Society, 88 *top;* Pioneer Hi-Bred International, Inc., 78–79; Payson D. Sheets, University of Colorado, 17; State of Illinois Department of Conservation, 92, 94–95, 97; US Department of Interior, National Park Service, Photo by Fred Mang, Jr., 106; William G. Winkler, 101, 102, 103, 104, 105.

1 2 3 4 5 6 7 8 9 10

Library of Congress Cataloging in Publication Data

Morrison, Velma Ford.
  Going on a dig.

  Includes index.
  SUMMARY: Presents an overview of archaeology, including how ancient sites become buried and are relocated and techniques of excavating. Relates information archaeology has revealed about Amerindians.
  1. Archaeology—Juvenile literature. 2. United States—Antiquities—Juvenile literature. 3. Indians of North America—Antiquities—Juvenile literature. 4. Excavations (Archaeology)—United States—Juvenile literature. [1. Archaeology. 2. United States—Antiquities. 3. Indians of North America—Antiquities. 4. Excavations (Archaeology)—United States] I. Title.
  CC171.M65   930.1'028   80–2776   ISBN 0–396–07915–6

FOR MY GRANDCHILDREN

Julie Morrison
David Morrison
Robert Morrison
Thomas Morrison
Mary Morrison
Mary Anderson
Nancy Anderson
Sarah Anderson
Anne Anderson
David Criner
Joel Criner
John Morrison
Hugh Morrison

Acknowledgments

I want to express my deep appreciation for the help I received in the development of this book. Wherever I went for assistance, whether to scholars in the field, to universities, to museums, or to the various state departments, I found interest and willingness to help.

I am especially indebted to Dr. Stuart Struever for giving so generously of his time and knowledge; and to Carol Stitzer, Del Baston, Dr. Harold Hutchinson, Dr. R. Bruce McMillan, and Sarah Criner for their many favors and cooperation in securing photographs for the book.

Velma Ford Morrison

Contents

1 A Jigsaw Puzzle 13
2 How Do You Know Where to Dig? 23
3 Archaeology—Old and New 31
4 A Fun Science 41
5 Kampsville 49
6 Koster 77
7 The Mound Builders 89
8 Dwellers in the Magnificent Southwest 99
9 The Search for America's Past Continues 113
Index 123

GOING ON A DIG

Archaeology in full swing at Koster site, Illinois

1
A Jigsaw Puzzle

Did you ever dig a hole in the ground to see what you could find? If so, what did you uncover? Was it a bone? An oddly shaped stone? A piece of colored glass? An arrowhead?

Did you wonder about what you found? Could you tell if the bone was that of an animal, bird, or human being? Did you wonder: Could the sharp edge of that stone have been used by someone long ago for cutting and scraping? Was that piece of colored glass a part of a vase? Or a window? How long had that arrowhead been buried there?

Trying to answer these questions is like trying to put together a jigsaw puzzle. It may be difficult, but it can sometimes be done. There is a science that teaches people how to solve the mysteries of things buried in the earth. It is called archaeology, from the Greek *archaeo,* meaning ancient or old, and *ology,* which means a study or a science. So we might say that archaeology is the study of ancient or very old things.

Men and women who study this science are called archaeologists. Like detectives, archaeologists are always looking for clues that might help solve the puzzle of how people lived thousands of years ago.

Artifacts excavated from the Illinois River Valley. Top to bottom: 3 deer antler tips used to flake edges of projectile points; bear tooth drilled to be strung into a necklace; obsidian projectile point, evidence of trade with other regions; copper awl for perforating skins; row of projectile points; and, top right, piece of pottery.

In ancient or prehistoric times, people did not read or write as they do now. They left no letters, no diaries, no history books. Yet they did leave a record of their way of life. Now buried in the earth, the record of this life is told in the remains of the things they left behind—skeletons, bones, teeth, trinkets, food, plants, tools, utensils, houses, carvings, and paintings.

Are you wondering: How did the past become a puzzle? How did so many prehistoric things become lost or buried? Nature has many ways of destroying and burying the past. Since earth first came into being, its surface has been undergoing constant change. It has been shaped by two kinds of action: by forces below the earth's surface or inside the earth, and by forces on the outside or surface of the earth.

14

Forces hidden inside the earth such as earthquakes can cause the ground to rise and fall like waves on the sea. Great cracks tear it open. Hillsides crash into rivers. Pieces of land sink, making long, narrow holes. Islands emerge or disappear, sandbars form or are washed away, shallow lakes evaporate and vanish, rivers and streams change their courses.

On the outside or surface of the earth, winds, water, and glaciers slowly cut away the land. They deposit sand, mud, and silt into streams, rivers, and lakes. With the passing of time, these materials form into thick layers of rock which lie upon one another. These rock layers are called strata.

Profile of sediments at an archaeological site shows the different strata.

Remains of plants and animals have been found preserved in the rock layers. These remains are called fossils. A fossil may be a whole skeleton, an outline of a body, a footprint, or even body tissue. Sometimes an entire animal or plant is preserved.

Through millions of years, tiny animals took calcium from the sea to form shells. As the animals died, the shells piled up. The weight of the shell layers pressed them together to form into limestone. Movements inside the earth pushed up the stone. As the limestone cooled, it changed into marble. In some of these slabs of marble, traces of ancient sea creatures can be seen.

A number of villages and cities were buried when a nearby volcano erupted and spilled ashes and lava over the land. Lava is the melted rock that pours out of volcanoes or from cracks in the earth. It is very, very hot, and sticky like molasses. But it cools and hardens quickly, forming a crust of rock. This lava rock preserves much of what becomes buried in it.

Climate is an important factor in the burying and preservation of the past. In tropical jungle areas where there is extreme heat and constant rain, plants grow very quickly. Abandoned settlements soon become buried by new growth that acts as a protective covering.

In very cold climates, frozen silts (very fine earth and sand carried by moving water) slowly covered the remains of prehistoric humans and animals. Miners in Alaska and hunters digging for buried ivory in Siberia have found re-

When a volcano erupts, the ashes and lava can bury whole villages or even a city.

mains of ancient hunting weapons and other tools in these frozen silts.

Dry sand and light, dry soil as well as peat bogs also have good preservative qualities. Many discoveries about bygone times have been made in sand-covered rubbish heaps of villages abandoned thousands of years ago. The dry sands of ancient Egypt buried and preserved the royal tombs in

17

Entrance to the Valley of the Kings, Egypt

the Valley of the Kings. In the desert regions of the state of Arizona, many ancient American Indian artifacts (human-made items) have been uncovered.

Sometimes the remains of villages and cities were buried on top of one another. To understand clearly how this could happen, let us imagine a few hundred prehistoric humans who lived in a particular area. Nearby was a gushing spring. A high bluff protected the valley from winds. It seemed an ideal spot. After some time, however, the food supply grew short and the people were afraid of starvation. So they decided to leave and search for a place where food was more plentiful. They took with them only what they could carry, leaving behind their dwelling places and many other possessions. With no one left to tend the land, it soon became overgrown with vegetation. Then, slowly, with the

18

passing of time, the winds and water began depositing mud, sand, and gravel upon the site where the village once had stood. Finally, the remains of the village became covered with a layer of light, dry soil, the type that has remarkable preservative qualities. In glancing over the site, a person could not tell that at one time a group of people had lived there.

Now, let us say that a thousand or more years pass. By that time nature had replenished the land. There were tall trees for fuel, and animals and fowl for hunting. Along came another group of people. When they saw the area, they decided to stay. There they lived in peace for many generations, until suddenly they were stricken with a killing disease. Within a short time the population was wiped out.

Archaeological sites are often discovered near springs or in river valleys.

Again the area became overgrown. Again, the winds and rains and floods washed in sand and gravel and mud. And again a prehistoric village became buried in the past.

Centuries later a third group of humans came upon the same place. They saw its many advantages. So the group settled there. Yet, this third village also was headed for disaster. A violent storm struck the area, and no one survived. Once more nature covered the land with a thick layer of earth. Once more an ancient village became buried.

Thus there came to be the remains of three different human groups or cultures buried upon the same site—each on top of the other like a huge layer cake! These buried layers that hold the remains of a certain group of people are called horizons. Archaeologists refer to each layer by number. For example, the top layer is called Horizon 1, the second from the top is Horizon 2, the third is Horizon 3, and so on. In some places as many as thirteen major horizons have been uncovered!

Nature is not the only thing guilty of destroying and burying the past. Human beings have done their share of destruction through wars, fires, and thievery. Many treasures have been looted by thoughtless, greedy persons. Others have been destroyed by ignorant people who did not realize the importance or value of their discoveries.

There is no way of telling what lies beneath a brush-covered land, a plowed field, or a tall building. It could be a human culture never before known—a culture whose burials might be a clue in answering the many questions archaeologists have been asking. For example:

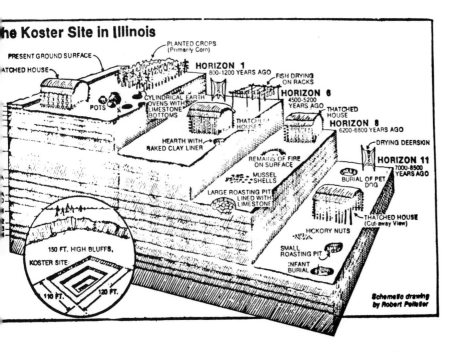

PLANTED CROPS
(Primarily Corn)

PRESENT GROUND SURFACE
ATCHED HOUSE

HORIZON 1
800-1200 YEARS AGO

FISH DRYING
ON RACKS

CYLINDRICAL EARTH
OVENS WITH
LIMESTONE
BOTTOMS

POTS

HORIZON 6
4500-5200
YEARS AGO

THATCHED
HOUSE

THATCHED
HOUSE

HORIZON 8
6200-6800 YEARS AGO

HEARTH WITH
BAKED CLAY LINER

DRYING DEERSKIN

REMAINS OF FIRE
ON SURFACE

HORIZON 11
7000-8500
YEARS AGO

MUSSEL
SHELLS

BURIAL OF PET
DOG

LARGE ROASTING PIT
LINED WITH
LIMESTONE

THATCHED HOUSE
(Cut-away View)

HICKORY NUTS

150 FT. HIGH BLUFFS,

KOSTER SITE

110 FT.   120 FT.

SMALL
ROASTING PIT

INFANT
BURIAL

Schematic drawing
by Robert Pelletier

Schematic representation of the horizons uncovered at Koster site in Illinois. Inset shows the complete hole. Drawing by Robert Pelletier.

Where did our early ancestors—the first humans—come from?

How old is the human species?

What did the first humans look like?

How old did they live to be?

When did humans first use fire? Invent tools? Create art?

What caused some cultures to die out? To disappear?

Such questions are of great interest to archaeologists. Trying to answer these questions is what archaeology is all about.

21

Burial mound in Illinois from the Middle Woodland period, about 100 B.C. *to* A.D. *400*

2
How Do You Know Where to Dig?

Are you wondering how archaeologists know *where* to dig? Or *where* to look? Do they simply take a spade and begin digging any place at all? No indeed. Unless they have some idea of where to start, they could spend a lifetime and never uncover a single artifact. Most often they have some sort of clue to guide them. Usually the site is a place where someone has already found bones, arrowheads, trinkets, shells, or bits of pottery.

To the trained eyes of the archaeologist, the type of land and the lay of the land are often clues. Many prehistoric peoples chose the great river valleys of the midwestern United States as the best place to live. Mounds constructed by these early humans may be found scattered throughout Middle America. Archaeologists are usually able to spot these mounds and the outline of bygone villages. Such places hold many secrets of the past.

River banks, dry rivers, lake beds, sea beds, and creek beds are also good places to dig or look for artifacts, especially after a storm.

Line of students searching a river bottom in Illinois. An unusual amount of cultural debris in a small area indicates a buried site on the shore nearby. BELOW: Pottery sherds recovered by the line of students.

In certain rocky areas, fossils may be found. (To a scientist, even sand is rock.) Some kinds of rock, such as granite, never contain fossils, while sedimentary rocks, such as shale, sandstone, siltstone, coal, and limestone, could have fossil bones entombed in them.

Other places worth checking are peat bogs, rock shelters, caves, and pit caves. For thousands of years, prehistoric humans inhabited rock shelters and caves, leaving behind

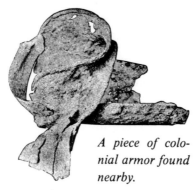

A piece of colonial armor found nearby.

LEFT: *Ruins of Jamestown, the first English town settled in America.*

fire pits, tools, shells, utensils, and the bones of the animals they ate. Pit caves are very deep holes or cracks in the earth. Many, many years ago animals and people sometimes fell to their deaths in these openings. Through the study of the remains preserved in such sheltered places, scientists are learning about the people and animals that once lived in the surrounding areas.

Often near historic sites such as battlefields, military and colonial relics can be found. A metal detector may be useful

Old print of temple in Yucatan

in locating items such as old coins, cannon balls, gun parts, and eating utensils. Of course metal detectors can only locate metal. Sometimes, however, when digging for metal objects, other objects are uncovered.

Through the study of history, old records, logs of ancient sailing ships, stories, and legends, many long-lost treasures have been found. For example, an eighteenth-century traveler's story of strange buildings in the jungles of Central America led two men to explore the area of Copán, Honduras. There, in 1839, these men discovered ancient Mayan ruins hidden under the dense jungle growth. Upon their return to the United States, the men published a book telling of their adventures. It was this book that encouraged others interested in archaeology to do more exploring of the ancient Mayan culture throughout Central America.

One of the strangest stories of all is that of a man named Heinrich Schliemann, who was born in Germany in 1822. At age seven he was given a book containing a picture of the burning of the ancient city of Troy. According to legend, the city had vanished without a trace of where it had once been. However, Schliemann found this hard to believe. There must be *some* clue to its whereabouts, he kept thinking. He decided to find the lost city of Troy. It would not be an easy task because he had no money. Furthermore, no one else believed the story in the book. But this did not discourage Schliemann. As soon as he was able, he began working at any job he could find. Being intelligent and a good worker, he soon found a position that paid well. When he had enough money, he went to Paris to study archaeology. Finally, in 1868, Schliemann, at age forty-six, was ready to set out to look for the lost city of Troy. Most people thought he was crazy.

One day when he was searching along the coast in Asia Minor, he came upon a flat-topped mound which met the description he had read in the book. With the help of one hundred hired men, he set to work digging. And low and behold! They uncovered nine horizons or buried cities, one

The hill of Hissarlik, situated in northern Asia Minor, was believed by Dr. Schliemann to be the site of Troy.

below another. But the most exciting part was yet to happen. Just the day before the work was to be finished, Schliemann and his wife came upon a pile of gold coins and artifacts. They decided to tell no one of their find. After sending away all their helpers, they set to work removing the treasures. Together they smuggled the gold out of Asia Minor. Many of the items they found were of great historic value. Like many treasure hunters, Schliemann, too, was greedy. However, his work did much to encourage interest in archaeology and ancient history.

Not all archaeological digging is done on land. Some is done under water. Scientists who specialize in this type of work are called underwater or undersea archaeologists. Throughout the ages, storms and battles have taken their toll of ships. Seas have flooded and buried whole towns. The work of the underwater scientist is to explore the remains of sunken ships and towns and to study everything found in the earth's waters, such as shells, plants, animal life, rocks, and soil. Thousands of items, some over two thousand years old, have been recovered from the water. This kind of work requires very special equipment. The divers wear masks, flippers, and breathing devices.

How do underwater archaeologists know where to "dig"? By studying historical records, accounts of storms and battles, and logs of ancient voyages, scientists can sometimes figure out approximately where a ship went down or a town was buried. Now and then fishermen pull objects from the sea which are a clue to the whereabouts of an underwater treasure. There are sonar-scanning devices that can survey

A rock shelter used as a campsite by prehistoric Midwestern Indians

large areas of the bottom of the sea from the surface. They can draw an electronic picture of everything lying on the sea floor. Another device helpful in locating underwater items is the magnetometer, which can locate metal.

Archaeological sites in the United States are more difficult to find than in most parts of the world. They are concealed and therefore harder to see. Many sites have already been destroyed by big earth-moving machines without anyone even knowing it was happening!

The United States Government has now passed laws which allow archaeologists to excavate a site before work is begun on the construction of dams, highways, and other large building projects. This government program is called "salvage archaeology."

But a person doesn't have to take part in a big dig, such as the excavation of a buried village or a sunken ship, in order to enjoy and participate in archaeology. Some of the most rewarding digs or treasure hunts are the little ones.

What a thrill it is to be poking around on a sandy beach and suddenly uncover a lovely, delicate sea shell! Or to be hiking along a creek bed after a storm and stumble upon a real honest-to-goodness Indian arrowhead! Or to be climbing along a rocky ledge and come upon a fern fossil!

Yes—the small, humble finds can be just as exciting as the grand ones.

3
Archaeology—
Old and New

No one knows exactly who the first archaeologist was. However, we do know that during the sixth century B.C. the king of ancient Babylonia excavated old buildings to find out who built them. And we know that Constantine the Great, about A.D. 330, sent an expedition to Palestine to try to locate and uncover the tomb of Jesus. The first persons who tried to find ancient works of art were not interested in archaeology but in money, because rich people would pay well for such treasures. No records were kept of where an artifact was found. Objects made of gold and silver were sometimes melted down and sold as metal. Those who came upon an ancient tomb simply threw away all except what could be sold. A great amount of archaeological material was destroyed in this way.

After the uncovering of Pompeii in the eighteenth century, more people began to take an interest in archaeology. Discovery in 1799 of the Rosetta Stone, which provided the key to the ancient Egyptian picture writing, was another step forward in arousing curiosity about ancient history. The work of Heinrich Schliemann in finding the lost city of Troy also helped to encourage interest in ancient cultures.

Old print shows Vesuvius in eruption, November, 1868. An earlier eruption in A.D. *79 totally destroyed the city of Pompeii.*

The Rosetta Stone, discovered in 1799, provided the key to Egyptian hieroglyphics.

In 1832, a Danish archaeologist named Christian Jürgensen Thomsen figured out how to separate and classify the different stages of human development in tool making. He classed them as the Stone Age, the Bronze Age, and the Iron Age. By 1900, most of the civilized world had become interested in archaeology. Universities, museums, and organizations such as the National Geographic Society and the Smithsonian Institution in the United States began sending out archaeological expeditions. In 1920, the tree-ring method of dating was discovered by an American astronomer, Andrew Douglass. This information helped archaeologists to find the age of a building by figuring out when the wood used in it must have been cut. Another happening that stimulated interest was the discovery of King Tutankha-

The earliest manufacture and polishing of flints, from a nineteenth-century book

mon's tomb in 1922. The tomb was filled with beautiful treasures, including the royal throne. Its discovery excited people all over the world.

The greatest breakthrough of all, however, occurred in 1949 with the discovery of radiocarbon dating by an American, Willard Libby. This method of dating makes use of atomic energy. All living things (as well as many nonliving things such as rocks) contain a certain amount of radioactive material called Carbon 14. By measuring the amount of radiocarbon in dead material, scientists can calculate how long the material has been dead. Thanks to this knowledge, scientists are now able to determine with some certainty the age of what they find at an archaeological site.

When most people think of archaeology, they picture someone dressed in helmet and shorts telling a group of native workers what to do. And every so often a hidden city with ruined temples full of treasures is uncovered. This kind of archaeology is becoming more and more a thing of the past. Many changes have taken place in recent years.

There are now two kinds of archaeology. One is called the old or classical; the other is called new or modern. Old or classical archaeology is the study of high civilizations that had complex forms of art, architecture, and writing. The cultures of ancient Greece, Rome, and Egypt are examples. The people of these cultures constructed great temples, produced elaborate works of art, and left a written record. The North American prehistoric cultures would not be considered high or classical because they developed no complex architecture or form of writing.

The rock temple at Abu-Simbel was excavated by high or classical archaeologists.

Classical archaeologists dig only a selected part of a site—the part that holds the treasure. They ignore the rest. They are more interested in things than people. In other words, they are interested in digging sites that show rather than those that tell. Classical archaeology came into being long before many scientific skills such as radiocarbon dating were known.

New archaeology came about with new discoveries in science. It began during the early 1950's at the University of Chicago as a branch of anthropology (the study of humans). It soon spread to other universities throughout the

35

New archaeologists study everything related to human life. Even a simple find tells a story about early people. Top row, from left to right: A carbonized wild grape seed, a fish scale, and a fish bone. Middle row: Walnut shell, snail shells. Bottom row: Carbonized pecan shells and fish bone. Penny is for scale.

United States where great schools of archaeology have been developed. Now it has even spread to Europe and other places in the world.

New or modern archaeology is quite different from the old or classical. New archaeology tries to explain *why* various cultures are different from one another and *why* they change. In addition to studying artifacts and other materials left by ancient people, new archaeologists examine

36

and study everything related to human life. They study the plants, animals, soil, rocks, and skeletons found at a site. They try to figure out what the environment was like in ancient times. From soil samples they can tell whether or not the soil has been disturbed for the past five hundred years! By studying pollen grains they can tell which trees, plants, shrubs, and grasses grew in an area. They can tell if a single tooth belonged to an ape or a human being. From a hipbone they can tell whether or not its owner walked erect. Even the humblest find—such as a broken clay bowl or a pile of shells—can tell a story about prehistoric people.

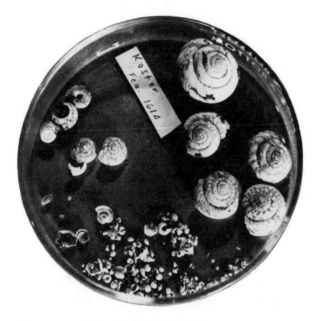

Land snails are sensitive to wet and dry habitats and can provide clues to prehistoric climatic fluctuations.

Perhaps you are thinking: Why should archaeologists study how human beings lived in ancient times except to satisfy their curiosity? What good will it do to find the answers to the questions? By studying the past we can learn many things which might help humanity now and in the future. For example, by studying the plants used as foods in prehistoric times, we might rediscover a forgotten native plant that could be cultivated and used as food for hungry people in the world today. Some plants that have been rediscovered and are now being researched by archaeologists in Illinois are pigweed, knotweed, goosefoot, marshelder, and acorns. *How* do we know for certain that these were used as food by humans in prehistoric times? We know because the seeds or remains of these plants were found in dried human feces (excrement) in caves and other places. It is now possible to analyze scientifically feces thousands of years old.

By studying bones and skeletons excavated from ancient cemeteries, new archaeologists are collecting information on diseases which can be very helpful to us in the future. They are trying to find out which human diseases are due to diet, living conditions, climate, or heredity. For example, the research now being done may someday help solve the mystery of the disease called arthritis.

Another question being studied by new archaeologists that might help humanity in the future is: What conditions lead to warfare? Is it overpopulation? Overuse of natural resources? If we could learn how to prevent wars and how to cope or live with our environment, think how wonderful that would be!

The exposed graveyard of an 800-year-old temple-mound community at Dickson Mounds Museum, Illinois. The remains are exactly as they were uncovered—including the goods buried with them.

We might say that new archaeology is actually many sciences all put together. It includes biology, zoology, botany, geology, anthropology, chemistry, and many, many others. It gives us facts—it gets our history correct, free from myths or untrue stories. It gives us a better understanding of ourselves and of the world in which we live.

4
A Fun Science

Archaeology can be a fun science, full of surprises and excitement. Further, it is one science in which amateurs or persons with little or no special training can take part and be a real help.

Some of the most important treasures in the world were not discovered by archaeologists but by amateurs—just ordinary people. For example, one day while digging in Egypt, a peasant woman unearthed the long-buried clay tablets that told the history of the fall of the Egyptian empire. The Rosetta Stone was discovered by one of Napoleon's soldiers. The lost city of Pompeii was found by an engineer who was digging an underground canal. Workmen laying a pipeline in Arizona discovered a buried Indian village. A farmer in Illinois uncovered shells, bones, and arrowpoints which led to the discovery of an ancient site containing thirteen different cultures. An alert rancher in Colorado plowed up some large bones which led to the discovery of the remains of an Ice Age bison kill. Discovery of the Folsom site—a very important one—in New Mexico was made by a Negro cowboy in 1925.

Not all discoveries have been made by adults. Many have

been made by children. Not long ago a young boy found bones which proved to be those of a mammoth, an animal now extinct. Many ancient hunting weapons and bones of extinct animals have been found by children in Alaska and Siberia. Other items unearthed by children which led to important discoveries are ancient tools of stone and bone, copper artifacts, pieces of pottery, arrowheads, beads, and coins.

But not all amateurs are trustworthy. Some are greedy. Others are ignorant. For example, in 1933, six amateur treasure hunters discovered an Indian mound in the state of

Many archaeological finds have been made by children. Here are fifth graders in Cedar Rapids, Iowa, working on a "simulated dig." Half the class makes artifacts and buries them. The other half excavates what was buried.

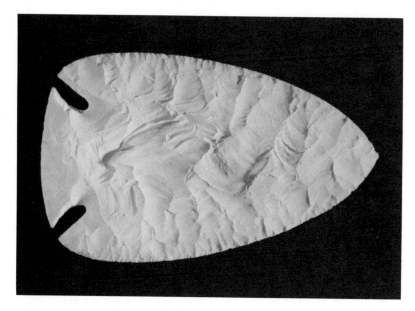

A finely crafted ceremonial projectile point recovered in a cache of Hopewell artifacts (mound builders).

Oklahoma. Instead of seeking scientific help, these men plundered the area. Not knowing the skills of digging, and not caring, they damaged many precious artifacts. Those they did not ruin, they sold on the spot at any price they could get. The rest they threw back upon the pile of dirt. As though that were not enough, they then blew up what remained so that all became lost to the world forever! What a shame that trained scientists were not on the scene of the digging to preserve the precious items and the information found in that burial chamber.

There is no way of knowing how many other valuable artifacts have been found and destroyed or sold by greedy

43

Beautiful ceremonial pipes shaped like animals made by prehistoric Indians about 2000 years ago

Pipe excavated in 1979

or ignorant persons. Robbers and treasure hunters are only interested in the artistic or commercial value of what they find, whereas archaeologists and scientists are interested in what they can learn from the things they uncover.

Since its beginning, the science of archaeology has been troubled by fakes and forgers as well as robbers and treasure hunters. We might ask: How can ordinary people—you—help to preserve important archaeological finds? Here is how:

1. Do not be a "pot hunter"—a person who ruins an artifact or a prehistoric site by careless digging. A pot hunter can do more damage than a bulldozer! An excavation is a very delicate operation. Each spoonful of earth must be checked carefully. (Chapter 5 will explain how the digging should be done).

2. If you find something you think might be important, report your discovery at once to an archaeologist, a state historical society, or the archaeology department of a university.

3. Do not "advertise" your find to people you cannot trust.

4. Refuse to buy or sell prehistoric artifacts.

5. Notify your State Department of Conservation immediately if you know of a site that is going to be destroyed.

6. If you have a collection, be sure it is properly identified and recorded.

The joy in archaeology is not in discovery alone. Working

Fossilized bones, teeth, and a tusk from American mastodon found in a Midwestern bog deposit

on a *real* dig or visiting one can be very exciting. Most people think of archaeological sites as being located only in foreign lands, and many travel to faraway places like Egypt, Yucatan, and Stonehenge to see them. But some of the most exciting digs are right here in the United States in our own back yards. For example, in the Black Hills of South Dakota, a group is excavating a graveyard of mammoths, extinct elephants, bears, coyotes, camels, and birds that were trapped in a limestone cave-in 22,000 years ago.

46

In Connecticut, another group is unearthing a Stone Age Indian camp. In Virginia and Pennsylvania, colonial plantations are being uncovered. Near Fort Myers, Florida, archaeologists are excavating a 6000-year-old cemetery where a thousand people were buried. There they are also digging up bones of extinct mammoth, bison, and ground sloth. Off the coast of Maine, underwater archaeologists are raising an ancient warship. Excavations are underway in almost every state, including Alaska.

Some of the most exciting sites of all are to be found in the state of Illinois. There lies the largest human-made prehistoric earthen construction in the world. There archaeologists have uncovered the remains of cultures that existed long before the pyramids were built in Egypt or Stonehenge in England. Who would ever have believed that buried under the cornfields of Illinois would be found such exciting things?

It takes a lot of time, money, and people to excavate an archaeological site. Good volunteers—people willing to

There are "digs" going on all over the United States. Here a group of volunteers launches a boat on the way to an island in the Illinois River for a day of excavating.

work for a while without pay—are needed to help scientists get the job done. We might ask: "What makes a good volunteer?" The answer: Someone who is trustworthy, alert, patient, full of curiosity, and able to stick with a job until it is finished.

Are you wondering how old a person must be in order to help on a real dig? It used to be thought that only college students or older persons were capable of assisting archaeologists. There was not a single program in the world that allowed young people to help. Scientists believed that children on a job would be a nuisance. However, there was one person—an Illinois schoolteacher named Genevieve MacDougall—who did not agree. She believed that certain youngsters of junior high school age were indeed capable of doing real archaeology. It was mainly through her efforts that Dr. Stuart Struever, head of Northwestern University's department of archaeology, decided to set up some short dig programs for junior high and high school students.

This program, which was begun in 1971, is the only one of its kind in the world today. It's the only one in which students twelve to fourteen years old are allowed to excavate real prehistoric sites under the supervision of professional scientists. The field school has been set up in the state of Illinois at a place known as Kampsville.

5
Kampsville

Kampsville is a small riverfront village in west central Illinois. It is named for Captain M. A. Kamp, one of its early citizens. It is very remote, nestled at the foot of steep bluffs in the floodplain between the Illinois and Mississippi rivers. No railroad leads to it. To this day, the only way

The only way to enter Kampsville from the east is by ferry.

to enter Kampsville from the east is by ferry boat. But the thing that makes Kampsville most unusual is that it lies in the midst of two thousand prehistoric communities and burial places. The village itself is built upon an ancient settlement.

Because of its location, Kampsville was chosen by Northwestern University and the Foundation for Illinois Archaeology as the place for their permanent archaeological research and teaching center. There are only two other such centers in the United States. These are located at Taos, New Mexico, and Vernon, Arizona. The Kampsville Center, however, is different from the other two. It is the only place that has a program for junior and senior high school students. And it's the only place where researchers are doing a complete and long-term study of more than ten thousand years of American Indian life in one area. They are gathering information on five hundred generations of *continuous* Indian life in the Illinois and Mississippi river valleys. This represents 99 percent of the time humans are known to have lived in this part of the world. Over the next twenty-

A group of junior high students arriving at Kampsville

The Kampsville Center offers programs for both adults and young people. Here young students excavate a cutbank while riverboat passes through channel in background.

five years, the scientists hope to excavate enough sites to give us the first complete and true picture of prehistoric Indian life in any area of the United States.

In addition to the junior and senior high school programs, the Kampsville Center offers field (dig) and laboratory programs for university and graduate students as well as dig programs for amateur adults. There are workshops for people who want to study Native American cultures. Those who take part in the latter program learn firsthand how people lived in prehistoric times. They gather raw materials from the surrounding area and learn how to make them into tools, clothing, and buildings. They learn to weave, make clay pots, and carve a canoe from a tree trunk. They go on wild food hunts, spending several days fishing and collecting wild plants, just as the Indians did thousands of years ago. The teachers at the Kampsville Center include specialists in human biology, zoology, botany, geology, min-

51

ing, engineering, physics, mathematics, computers, and anthropology.

There are twelve scientific laboratories, an archaeological library, and a museum. A salvage archaeology operation is also stationed at the Kampsville Center. More than twenty scholars and technicians work to rescue archaeology in the area.

In Kampsville, everyone has come to do archaeology. Archaeology is everywhere. Students from all over the United States and Canada study there. Some return for a second, third, and even fourth summer. It is indeed an unusual learning place. In most schools, students sit in a classroom and *read* about archaeology and how to dig a site. At Kampsville, students *do* the archaeology and *do* the digging.

At Kampsville the junior high students stay in an old remodeled farmhouse located within walking distance of the village. Boys live on one side of the house and girls

Older students use buckets to remove water and mud from their excavation after a hard rain.

RIGHT: *View of the Sniader Center, a remodeled farmhouse where junior high students live at Kampsville*

Every evening after supper there are lectures, games, or slides. Here students attend a lecture in the "Barn," a hayloft converted into a meeting room.

A group of junior high students gather in front of a dorm.

on the other. Nearby is the "Barn." Its loft has been made into a recreational and meeting room. The downstairs or lower level is used as a place for teaching pottery making, finger weaving, tool making, and other crafts. Back of the farmhouse rise beautiful high bluffs—an ideal place for climbing and exploring. There one can find chert (a type of stone used for tool making), clay for pottery making, shells, and even Indian artifacts.

Besides the teachers and leaders, in the junior high program there is a chaperone—usually a parent—for every seven or eight students.

The junior high program at Kampsville is *real* archaeology. It includes far more than just learning how to dig a site. Each day the program is different. Much of it depends upon the weather, special events, and what is found at the different sites.

Before the students go into the field they are taught a few basic things about archaeology. For example, there are a number of words for which they must learn the meaning. In addition to those already defined, here are some others:

Educational sessions are part of lab work. Students must be trained in lab before they are permitted to work in the field so they know what to look for and how to excavate. Field and lab work are conducted on alternate days.

Datum post in lower righthand corner of square is used for measuring.

ANTHROPOLOGY	The study of people
DATA	Facts or information gathered from a dig site
DATUM POST	Post at corner of square used for vertical measuring
DEBRIS (da *bree*)	Anything left behind at an archaeological site, including human-made and natural objects
FAUNA	Animals living in a certain region at a certain time
FORMS	Special forms for notes and map to record information while "charting" a square

LINE LEVEL	Instrument used to show whether site is level
LITHICS	The study of stone tools
MIDDEN	The layer of refuse left at a site
SHERD	A broken piece of pottery
SITE	Any place where people lived and worked
SQUARE	Square area marked off for digging
STERILE SOIL	Soil that contains no debris from human occupation
TARP	Protective covering for square

Student has finished excavating a three-inch level and is "charting" it on the proper form.

Tarped squares wait for another dig day. Note tarp rocks.

TARP ROCKS	Rocks for holding down protective covering over a site
TEMPER	Material added to clay in making pottery. Temper prevents pottery from exploding when being fired. Crushed rock, ground-up sherd, shells, or grass can be used.

The students are told the history of the different cultures or groups of people who lived in the Illinois River Valley during prehistoric times. They are shown slides and movies of the different kinds of houses, tools, and pottery that these early people had. They are shown actual artifacts from early cultures. Then, when they go on a real dig, they will be able to identify the artifacts they uncover.

The junior and senior high students have their own sites

Mornings begin with a good breakfast. The interior of Kampsville Center dining hall.

to dig. On a typical "dig" day (they do not dig every day) they get up early in the morning and walk to the village for breakfast. It is served in the Kampsville Center's dining hall, a very pleasant place built in 1977 with money raised by donations. It seats 150 people. After breakfast the students are taken by bus to their excavation sites.

Students head for the bus to take them to their excavation sites.

Digging is a science. Great care must be taken if it is to be done right. There is an instructor for every five or six students. The first thing the students learn is *safety* in the field. The rules are:

1. Never lean on datum posts.
2. Never step or sit on the edge of the square.
3. Never throw tarp rocks.
4. Never run on the site.
5. Never leave shovel or trowel blades sticking up.

The instructors explain how a site is put together. They show the students how the measuring, mapping, digging, and note keeping should be done. The digging is done in

A test square being charted carefully. When an entire area cannot be excavated, statistical analysis of things found in the test square will serve as well for information purposes as if entire site were excavated.

Students measuring a square

six-foot squares in levels three inches deep. Students do their own measuring and mark off their squares. Every square is given a number. Everything that comes out of a particular square must be labeled with the site name, square number and level, excavator's name, description of the item, and location and condition in which it was found.

Note trowel student is using on the wall of a test trench.

A soft brush is useful for clearing dirt from fragile things.

Various tools and equipment are used in archaeological digging. Some of them are: shovel, trowel, pick, spoon, tweezers, bamboo pick, soft brush, nylon string, line level, centimeter ruler, bushel basket, bags, tags, note forms, and map forms.

The instructors explain when and how each tool should be used. In digging, great care must be taken so as not to damage any artifacts or debris. Objects are never to be yanked out of a square. Tiny objects may be lifted with tweezers. The bamboo pick, a thin and sharp durable stick, is useful in separating delicate items, and the soft brushes for clearing dirt from fragile things.

It's important to take into account the condition of materials before trying to remove them. Bone may be hard or it may be crumbly; shell may be chalky or flaky. So a person should try not to touch a bone or shell with the fingers, a shovel, or a trowel. Instead, without touching the material, the surrounding dirt should be loosened gently with a small trowel or the fingers until the object is exposed. An experienced person such as an instructor should then examine the object to determine the best method for its extraction. If it is in good, solid condition, it can probably be lifted gently by hand. But if it is crumbly, it may be necessary to spray it first with a clear cellulose glue. This procedure will help hold the parts together. There is no one master method of excavation. Just remember to use common sense.

Here are some important pointers to keep in mind while digging:

1. Do not remove bones or other objects from the ground until you've checked their relationship to each other. Take great care to see if the bones you find close to each other could be from the same animal or from different animals.

2. Examine each bone and shell carefully for any changes in them that could have been made by human hands. Has the bone or shell been burned? Has the bone or shell been made into or used as a tool? Look for polish on all parts of the bone. Has it been shaped into a point? Is it notched? Does the bone have cut or scratch marks on its surface? If you've been careful in your digging,

Students carefully expose shells of mussels. They use soft brushes to loosen the dirt, after noting the position of shells on the chart of the square. Later all the information can be reassembled like a scientific jigsaw puzzle.

Pottery vase recovered from 1000-year-old cemetery by Northwestern University archaeologists.

you will know whether such marks are the result of your trowel or shovel or of something that the people who once lived at the site were doing.

3. Be alert to note any changes in soil color. Dark charcoal-colored dirt lying in light-colored soil could mean that at one time that place had been used for a fire pit.

4. If you find a broken piece of pottery, note if it has concave or convex sides. Examine the broken edge of the sherd to see if you can tell which type of temper was used in its firing.

5. Examine each stone for changes that might have been made by humans. Examine the edges for flake scars; corners for any pecking; faces for grooves; and the sides for angles and smoothness.

Soil-color changes and the exact position of everything found in a square must be marked on a map and described

65

Each student is given a basket in which to toss excavated dirt.

in notes using the proper forms. Each student is given a basket in which to toss the excavated dirt and a bag to hold the material found.

Very small objects are sometimes overlooked during digging. To make certain that none are missed, the dirt from the baskets is dumped on a wire screen. Objects one-half inch or larger are thus caught on the screen.

To rescue seeds, nutshells, fish scales, and pieces of animal remains, the dirt is gently poured into water. Any items lighter than water will float to the top and can be lifted out with a tea strainer. This process is called flotation.

After being labeled and tagged, items are washed and

66

Screening in the field. BELOW: *Closer view of screening process.*

The students wash their own artifacts.

placed on racks to dry. Students wash their own artifacts. They learn to identify limestone, chert, pottery, and other things they find in their field.

Some people may think that once something is found and dug up, the work of the archaeologist is ended. Nothing could be further from the truth. The finding of debris and artifacts is only the beginning. At Kampsville, after the materials have been washed, dried, and tagged, they are sorted into different groups and sent to one of the many labs to be analyzed and studied. The animal remains are

Once something has been dug up, the work has only begun. ABOVE: Students list and describe artifacts and cultural debris. Charts and level forms are very important for future analysis of site history. BELOW: The washed artifacts and cultural debris are tagged and put into plastic bags to be studied by researchers. The Kampsville collection is permanently maintained.

Junior high school group on dig day

sent to the zoology lab; the plant remains to the botany lab; bones to the osteology lab; pollen to the pollen lab; and rocks to the geology lab. There is also a computer lab.

Sometimes the students will dig in the morning, and some-

"Tarping" the squares

At the end of the dig day, students turn in their "level forms" and bagged cultural debris.

times in the afternoon. At the close of each dig session, the students cover their squares with tarpaulins or waterproof material for protection from weather, animals, and birds. Then they clean their tools, tie their debris bags, check their notes, and turn everything over to one of the instructors. If a dig session is held in the morning, a picnic lunch is usually taken to the site by the teachers. Between

71

forty-five minutes and an hour is spent in eating, visiting, and relaxing. Then the students and instructors board the bus for their return to the village.

In the junior high program, a part of each day is devoted to some project related to archaeology. The students learn to make ceramics as the Indians did in prehistoric times. They dig their own clay from the bluffs back of the dorm and they fire their own pottery. They learn how the introduction of pottery affected the lives of prehistoric people.

Another subject covered in the program is lithics, and

LEFT: *Lining up for lunch at the dig site*

Part of each day is devoted to some project related to archaeology. RIGHT: *Pottery makers.* BELOW: *Students experiment at shaping flint into projectile points and tools by stiking or pecking off flakes from the stone.*

Kampsville dining hall. Everyone gathers there for supper.

the students consider the effect stone tools had on early people, too. Students soon learn to recognize chert or flint and other materials used in tool making.

Zooarchaeology—the study of animal bones found at an archaeological site—is discussed, and students learn about the different animals that lived in the Illinois River Valley during prehistoric times.

Other programs include the study of plants, nutrition (the foods eaten by prehistoric people), geology, weaving, and thatching.

For the junior group, all programs end about three o'clock in the afternoon. At that time the students enjoy a shower and a change of clothing. After that there is time to relax— to play a game of horseshoes, to walk to the village for an ice cream treat, to go to the "Barn" and listen to records, or to explore the bluffs above the village.

At supper time everyone gathers at the Center's dining hall. The menu includes plenty of fresh vegetables and fruits. Teachers and students alike help with the local harvesting. They pick for neighboring farmers "on shares," which means that for every three or four bushels of produce they pick, they get to keep one for the Kampsville Archaeological Center's kitchen.

Every evening after supper there are lectures, games, and the showing of slides. The lectures cover such topics as carbon dating, the study of skeletons, and ancient Indian cultures.

Instructor John White tells students stories handed down to him by his Cherokee Indian forefathers.

Students can hardly wait to crawl into their bunks. Though they are tired, they feel good about their day.

By about nine-thirty or ten, everyone's eyelids begin to grow heavy. The students can hardly wait to crawl into their bunks. Though they are tired, they feel good about their day. Yes, Kampsville is a different way of life. It's archaeology—sure. But it's also much more. It's learning about yourself, it's making friends, it's a feeling of pride, it's unforgettable—and it's fun! At Kampsville, archaeology is not just what you find—it's what you find out.

6
Koster

The greatest and most important archaeological site yet discovered in North America lies just a few miles from Kampsville. For many years, people in this area have found artifacts in their fields, gardens, creek beds, and along the river banks—especially after a storm. The land belonging to a farmer named Theodore Koster seemed to have an especially large number of arrowheads, pottery pieces, and other artifacts buried in its soil. It was from the Koster farm that amateur archaeologist Harlan Helton took some arrowheads and pieces of pottery to show Stuart Struever at Northwestern University. After questioning Helton about the artifacts, Dr. Struever's curiosity was aroused. He decided to visit the Koster farm.

To the average person, Koster's farmland looked like any other Illinois cornfield. But Dr. Struever's trained eyes noticed the lay of the land. There was shelter from the winds by high bluffs. There was a spring nearby which supplied water the year around. It was an ideal site for a settlement. As soon as he began walking down the corn rows, Dr. Struever saw numerous pieces of pottery on the ground. He recognized these as being from a 1000-year-old culture

Who would believe that under this cornfield nine levels of human history might be found?

called Jersey Bluff. Then he came across artifacts from earlier cultures. The more he studied the area, the more he became convinced that one or more prehistoric villages lay buried under that cornfield. He asked Mr. Koster's permission to dig some test pits.

The following summer, 1969, Dr. Struever and a group of students from Northwestern University began digging in the Koster field. Before the summer was over, they knew they had found one of the greatest archaeological sites of

78

all times. They decided to name it for the kind and generous couple, Mary and Theodore Koster, upon whose land the discovery was made.

Koster is the largest and most complex archaeological excavation ever undertaken in America. Thirteen major horizons have been uncovered! And there may be more. As yet, no one knows for sure. The water level makes it impossible to dig further without special, expensive equipment.

Why is the Koster site so important? It is important be-

79

cause it covers more than ten thousand years of continuous human history. Over seven thousand years before Christ was born, at least five thousand years before Stonehenge was built, and more than four thousand years before the great pyramids of Egypt were erected, humans with a well-developed culture were living upon the land where Koster's cornfield stood! Never before has a site been found where the soil was more favorable for preserving animal and plant remains. From the things found there, scientists are finally learning the true story of some of the first people of North America. They are solving the mysteries of how the early peoples of the Illinois River Valley lived: what they ate, how their tools were made and used, what diseases they suffered, how they built their homes, and how they buried their dead.

These Koster people were the ancestors of today's American Indians—or Amerindians, as they often are called now. We know this from the scientific study of the human skeletons found during the digs. From the excavations, we have learned that these natives of America were clever, intelligent people. They were able to think and carry out complex plans for getting food and raw materials from their environment. As far back as 8400 years ago, they had acquired technical skills in woodwork, basket weaving, and plant processing.

They made good tools and kept improving them.

They were not nomads—people always on the move in search of food—as once thought. They lived in very small villages, probably in semi-permanent houses. Evidence of

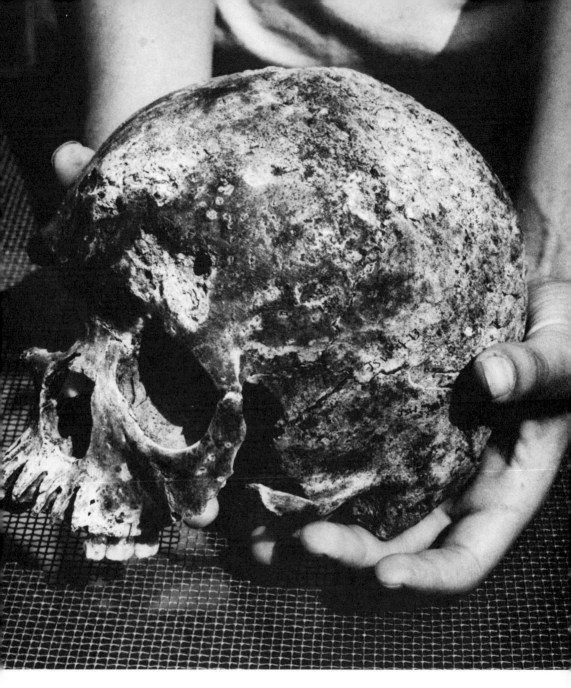

Human skull excavated from Illinois valley

the earliest permanent houses yet found in North America was discovered at Koster Horizon 8, dated 5000 B.C. These were built on human-made terraces. The walls of the houses were made of woven twigs covered with mud plaster, and roofs were thatched.

These early Amerindians took care of their old people. They honored their dead and buried them in a special way. The earliest human cemetery yet found in eastern North America was discovered at Koster Horizon 11 (6400 B.C.). The bodies had been placed in oval pits with their knees drawn up to their chests. Some of the graves had been covered with large stones.

The skeleton of an 18-month-old baby, from soil dated 5100 B.C., was found covered with powdered red ocher. This find was a surprise to archaeologists. They knew this burial practice was common in America at a much later date. But they had never heard of it's being done in such ancient times.

At Koster, care was even taken with the burial of some animals, which were probably pets. The remains of three dogs, each appearing to have been buried with special ceremony, were found. A drawing was discovered at Koster showing a woman with a basket of hickory nuts returning to the village with a dog—evidence of dogs for pets. No one knows when dogs first appeared in North America. The oldest bones so far are those dated 5100 B.C. discovered at Koster.

It used to be thought that these prehistoric people were big game hunters and eaters. But they weren't. They de-

This dog was buried about 6000 years ago at the Koster site. It was a domestic dog, and had died a natural death. No one knows why it was buried with its head resting on and against grinding stones. A mussel shell lies nearby, exactly as it was uncovered by the archaeologist, John Hewitt. To the right is a bamboo pick, thin, strong, sharp, and useful for excavating small fragile materials.

pended more on plants than animals for food. The Illinois River Valley was not a place of hardship. For food, there were hickory nuts, cereal-like seeds, duck potatoes, water lotus, goosefoot, and many other edible plants; also fish, ducks, geese, rabbits, and white-tailed deer.

Men and women shared in the work. The women gathered the nuts and seeds, and fished. The men did the hunting. In the fall they used dogs, running the deer until the animals were exhausted and then killing them with spears. The men also caught ducks and other fowl.

Deer were roasted and fish smoked in huge pits fifteen feet in diameter. Grinding stones weighing forty pounds were used for processing nuts.

There is evidence that, about 3900 B.C., the Koster people began carrying on trade with other groups. Obsidian (a dark, glass-like rock) found in the ruins was traced to Yellowstone Park, more than a thousand miles away! Also, copper from the northern Great Lakes and mica and beads from the southern Appalachians were found.

The greatest changes in human life for the Koster people occurred during the Horizon 1 occupation (A.D. 400–1000). It was during this period of time that pottery replaced woven fiber containers. The bow and arrow replaced the spear. Full-scale cultivation of maize (corn), squash, and beans began. The first large town or community came into being. Religious motifs made their appearance. And for the first time, warfare came to Koster! We know because during the excavation of the Horizon 1 cemetery, archaeologists

Close-up of charred woven fabric 1400 years old, found in the Illinois River Valley. Material had been rolled up, thus protecting the inner part.

found arrowheads embedded in many of the skeletons—evidence of human fighting.

Each horizon tells a story about the people who once lived there. Each is a chapter in the long history of human effort for survival and improvement. The very earliest Koster inhabitants might be called the hunting-gathering people; the later ones, the agriculture people.

The Koster excavation programs under the direction of Dr. Struever lasted ten years. They finally came to a close in 1979. The archaeological teams then turned their efforts to other important sites in the Kampsville area.

There are no great monuments or ruins to see at Koster.

85

Part of the "hole" at Koster

Now it is just an ordinary grainfield. The huge excavated hole itself—a 40,000-square-foot, L-shaped pit that once contained the remains of many human groups or cultures buried at the same site one upon another—has been filled with earth. Here, over a span of more than ten thousand years, people came, spent their lives, and disappeared as the wind and soil covered their villages until the next ones arrived. The story of Koster, then, is the story of people and how they lived their daily lives thousands of years ago.

From the Koster site, scientists have learned many important facts about Native Americans and human development. Scientists believe that the remains of many other cultures we know nothing about lie waiting to be discovered in the Illinois River Valley. If this is true, Koster could be the beginning—not the end.

ABOVE: *Serpent Mound, Ohio*. BELOW: *Little Bear Mound, Iowa*.

7

The Mound Builders

Scattered throughout the central and eastern United States are thousands of prehistoric, human-made mounds. More than ten thousand have been found in Ohio alone! They are all sizes and shapes. Some are square, some are round, and some are oval. Some are formed in the shape of humans, animals, and birds. One, called Serpent Mound, is 1300 feet long and covers sixty acres of ground. It is made of stone and clay in the shape of a coiling snake with its jaws wide open. It's the largest effigy mound in the world. (An effigy is an image of some living thing— for instance, a statue.) Another example is Rock Eagle Effigy Mound in Georgia, an eagle with wings spanning 120 feet. In southern Wisconsin there are five thousand human and animal effigy mounds in the shapes of eagles, buffalo, elk, moose, deer, wolves, and panthers. Some of the panthers have tails 350 feet long, and some of the wing spans of the eagles measure a thousand feet. Many of the oldest mounds are made of sea shells. Fig Island Shell Ring in South Carolina, built about four thousand years ago, is among the oldest in North America.

About fifty miles south of Kampsville, Illinois, lies Ameri-

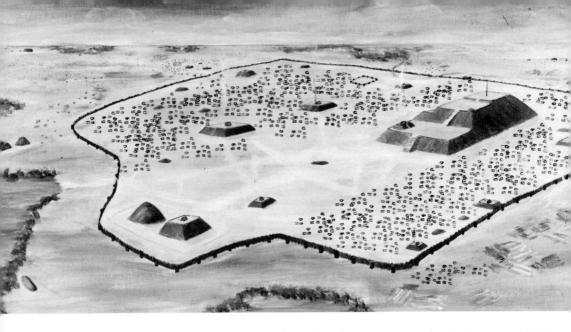

An artist's drawing of Cahokia during the Moorehead phase, A.D. *1150–1250.*

ca's first prehistoric city north of Mexico. It is called Cahokia for the Cahokia Indians of the Illinois Nation. It covered six square miles and had a population of more than forty thousand people, which was very great for such ancient times. It was the main center for the Mississippian Culture. In this ancient city of Cahokia is the largest prehistoric earthen construction in the world—its base is even larger than Egypt's great pyramid! It covers sixteen acres of ground. It is so big that many people thought it must have been built upon a natural hill. But scientific tests have proved that it is all human made and that it was built in fourteen different stages. Called Monks Mound, it was named for some monks who lived in that area from 1808 until 1813.

Monks Mound once stood in the midst of more than one hundred smaller mounds. Of these, forty have been preserved. The rest have been destroyed by modern farming methods and by the construction of highways, stores, and homes. Only the central part of the great prehistoric city of Cahokia is left, and it is preserved by the State of Illinois.

The main Cahokian mounds were flat on top and made entirely of earth. The soil was broken up with digging tools made of wood, shell, or stone and carried in handwoven baskets to the construction site. On the top of Monks Mound once stood a massive building at least 105 feet long and 50 feet high. It was used as the home for chiefs and priests. On top of the other mounds were temples and other build-

Artist's drawing of Monks Mound shows large building and stockade on top.

Burial site exhibit

ings for ceremonial and religious purposes. In one of the smaller mounds excavators found the burial site of a man about forty-five years of age. He must have been a very important person—a chief or ruler—because he had been laid out on a blanket or cape decorated with more than twenty thousand mother-of-pearl beads cut from Gulf of Mexico conch shells! Near him were other burials with other

92

foreign treasures such as rolls of copper from the Great

Lakes area, mica from the Carolinas, and more than eight hundred beautiful arrowheads made of flint from different parts of the Midwest. This find is evidence that the Cahokians had contact with other groups of people. Imagine the labor and the engineering ability it must have taken to construct these great mounds by hand—without the help of modern machinery and tools!

The prehistoric people of Cahokia even understood many things about the science of astronomy. Archaeologists have excavated four circular sun calendars at Cahokia. These sun calendars were probably used to predict the changing seasons. The name "Woodhenge" has been given to them

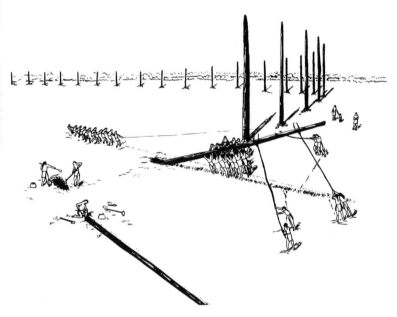

Artist's drawing of Woodhenge at Cahokia, a circular sun calendar much like Stonehenge.

Photo of mound at Cahokia, Illinois. Note excavation site at top fore-ground of mound.

Closer views of dig site, Cahokia

because they are so much like Stonehenge in England. Instead of being made of stone, however, at Cahokia the posts were wooden logs, evenly spaced in perfect circles.

The Cahokians were noted not only for their engineering ability and knowledge of astronomy but also for their fine works of art. We know this because in and near the mounds archaeologists have discovered beautiful ceramics, wood carvings, fine pieces of stone work, and embossed copper sheets.

The early European settlers in America puzzled over these peculiar earthen mounds. *Who* were the mound builders and *why* did they build the mounds? they wondered. The early settlers did not believe that the huge earthworks could have been built by the Indians. They did not think that such "primitive" people as the tribes seemed to them were capable of constructing anything so great. They also did not believe the Amerindians capable of having created the great works of art found in and near the mounds. They decided that some foreign "civilized" race—perhaps the Egyptians—had somehow reached America and done the building.

In recent years, archaeological research has done much to solve the mystery of the mounds. The truth is that these mounds scattered throughout the United States were not built by the Egyptians or any other so-called "superrace." They were built by the American Indians—ancestors of the Creeks, Cherokees, Natchez, and the other Indian tribes that first greeted the white people from Europe. We know now that the mounds were built by different Indian cultures

Archaeological site showing the different strata, Cahokia

at different times. Most of them date within 2500 years before Columbus came to America. We also know that they were constructed for different purposes. Some were burial places; some were altars; some, boundary markers. Others were fortifications, or foundations for houses and other buildings.

The mound builders were capable, intelligent people. They built thriving towns. They created a network of trade that reached from the Great Lakes to the Gulf of Mexico. Their

97

works of art can compare with the finest of European civilizations. These mound builders were farmers. Their fields stretched for miles. Their main crops were corn, beans, and squash.

By studying postholes, bits of pollen, and various buried artifacts found at the mounds, archaeologists are at last piecing together the true story of the mound builders.

Perhaps somewhere there lies another brush-covered "hill"—another Monks Mound—with its burials untouched; one that can tell us more about these vanished people. If so, let us hope it will be discovered by an archaeologist and not by a pot hunter!

8

Dwellers in the Magnificent Southwest

Some of the most magnificent prehistoric ruins in the United States are in the Southwest—in Colorado, New Mexico, and Arizona.

Hundreds of years ago, long before white people came to America, Indians living in southwestern Colorado built their homes along overhanging walls of canyons for protection against other tribes. Some of the homes were built in the open, but many were in caves, where they were well protected from the weather. By studying the remains found in and around these dwellings, archaeologists have been able to piece together the story of the life and customs of the people who once lived there.

The cliff dwellers, as they are now called, were short and black haired. The backs of their heads were flat because, as babies, they were carried on hard cradleboards. This caused their soft young bones to become permanently flattened. Their homes were often four, five, and even more stories high. The rooms were small and oblong in shape and built in a stair-step design. They were stacked one upon another, with each room set back a few feet from the room beneath it so that the roof of one would be the front yard of the one above it. There were no doors or windows on the ground floor. The roofs were reached by ladders. In case enemies attacked, the ladders could be drawn up, and the people would fight from their house tops. The structure was like a big apartment house with many people living there. It was a village in itself.

Each village had round underground chambers called kivas which were entered by ladders through openings in the roofs. Kivas were used for religious ceremonies and as clubhouses for the men. The walls were usually decorated with paintings in earth colors of red, yellow, and green.

These cliff dwellers were good farmers. They grew corn, squash, beans, cotton, and tobacco. Their bowls and dishes were beautifully decorated. Their tools were made of bone and flint, and their weapons of polished stone.

For eight-hundred years, these peace-loving people built their cliff dwellings and farmed their lands. Then a strange thing happened. They all began moving away, leaving most of their possessions behind. Why did they leave? Where did they go? No one knows for certain. Some archaeologists believe that a long drought drove them away. Without water, the people could not survive. They were forced to leave their homes and many of their possessions and seek new places in which to live.

Other archaeologists believe that the people were forced away because of frequent enemy attacks. Whatever the reason, everyone left. Many centuries went by. Then, one wintry day in 1888, two cowboys exploring southwestern Colorado came upon an unbelievable sight. Up high in a cave along the overhanging walls of a canyon they saw what appeared to be a huge white palace. Imagine their surprise at seeing such a sight in the middle of nowhere! Before long they knew they had discovered an ancient cliff dwelling. They named it Cliff Palace.

Cliff Palace is the largest and best-preserved prehistoric cliff dwelling in the world today. It rises eight stories high and contains more than two hundred rooms. The flat roofs are gone, but the walls of the rooms, twenty-three kivas,

Two cowboys exploring southwestern Colorado came upon this unbelievable sight. They called it Cliff Palace. (Mesa Verde National Park)

Two views of the Long House, Mesa Verde National Park

and a number of storage bins are still standing. Among the ruins were hundreds of artifacts—bows and arrows, clothing, food, jewelry, and even some mummies of the people themselves. Many of the artifacts have been placed in the state museum in Denver.

The area around Cliff Palace is known as Mesa Verde, which is the Spanish for "green table." It was given this name because it is covered with many green juniper and pinion trees. Besides Cliff Palace, there are many other interesting archaeological sites to see at Mesa Verde. These include Sun Temple, Balcony House, Cedar Tree House, and a place called Long House which was first opened to the public in 1973. It is built in a huge rock shelter. It has 150 rooms and 21 kivas. Mesa Verde is actually an enormous

The Sun Temple, Mesa Verde National Park

LEFT: *An aerial view of the Sun Temple, Mesa Verde National Park,* and ABOVE: *A close-up. Note the round kivas.*

outdoor archaeological museum full of wonderful, exciting things to see.

One of the most impressive archaeological sites in the United States lies about one hundred miles south of Mesa Verde on the desert floor in Chaco (*Cha*h-koh) Canyon, New Mexico. It is called Pueblo Bonito, which means beautiful town or village. It was first discovered in 1849 by U.S. soldiers passing through New Mexico. However, excavation of the site was not begun until seventy-two years later, in 1921. The digs were sponsored by the National Geographic Society under the direction of Smithsonian archaeologist Neil Judd. It took seven years and seven expeditions to complete the work.

105

U.S. soldiers discovered Pueblo Bonito in Chaco Canyon, New Mexico, in 1849.

Pueblo Bonito is the most remarkable structure ever erected by prehistoric Native Americans north of Mexico in the area now called the United States. It is actually a city built in the form of a huge apartment house around inner courtyards. It contains eight hundred rooms and once housed twelve hundred people. It is the largest prehistoric apartment house in the world. Its outer walls rise four stories high and have no windows or doors. The only way in or out of this ancient "city" was by ladder. Huge logs were used for house beams. These were cut with stone axes. Many of the walls were built of cut and shaped stones, so perfectly fitted they needed no mortar! Outside the walls were ridges built of earth for trapping water that came down from the mesas. The water was used for irrigation and other purposes. Many large and small kivas were unearthed.

Among the ruins at Pueblo Bonito, archaeologists found some of the most beautiful prehistoric pottery known. It is decorated with thin black lines against a white surface. Handsome ornaments and jewelry made of turquoise and shell were found also. One, a breathtaking turquoise necklace, is made of 2500 beads! Imagine the hours of labor it must have taken to form each individual bead by rubbing it smooth with a block of sandstone and then to pierce a hole in it by drilling with a handmade tool. This necklace was found buried with four turquoise ear pendants under fifteen feet of sand! These beautiful pieces of pottery, ornaments, and jewelry have been placed in museums.

Other artifacts found at Pueblo Bonito were sandals made of fiber, woven blankets, clothing of tanned skin, grinding stones, and cooking pots.

Archaeologists believe that at one time as many as five thousand people lived in and around Chaco Canyon. It took a lot of food, wood, and other natural resources to support so many. With the passing of time, life in the canyon became more and more difficult. Finally there was no wood left for fuel or building. All the forests on the mesas had been used up. Without trees to hold the moisture in the ground, erosion occurred. Crops would not grow. Famine set in, and the people left. Windblown sand and dust gradually filled the great buildings. Some became completely covered. They looked like huge hills. Thus the story of the magnificent Pueblo Bonito came to an end.

There are hundreds of other archaeological sites besides Pueblo Bonito in Chaco Canyon. However, most have not been excavated. They are being saved for future archaeologists to study.

One of the most unusual prehistoric sites in the Southwest is near Santa Fe, New Mexico, in Frijoles Canyon. There, during the late 1800's, an archaeologist named Adolf Bandelier (Ban-duh-*leer*) discovered carved stone mountain lions unlike anything found elsewhere in the United States! In the canyon he also discovered an ancient settlement and a huge cave with prehistoric paintings in color on the rocks.

One of the most famous archaeological discoveries was made in 1927 near Folsom, New Mexico. There, a Negro cowboy found a spearpoint between the ribs of a bison skeleton of a type that had long been extinct. It was this find that proved beyond a doubt that humans were living in America twelve to fourteen thousand years ago. Later a

The carved stone mountain lions found by archaeologist Adolf Bandelier during the nineteenth century in New Mexico

discovery of a different kind of spearpoint, near Clovis, New Mexico, proved that humans were living there even earlier than fourteen thousand years ago.

The state of Arizona also contains many archaeological wonders. Sixty miles north of the town of Flagstaff is a place called Dinosaur Canyon, where footprints left by huge dinosaurs can be seen in the white sandstone.

Deep in a canyon on the Navajo Indian Reservation in northern Arizona are three outstanding cliff dwellings. One, called Betatakin (Be-*tah*-tah-kin) in the Navajo language, meaning ledge house, is built in a sandstone cave almost five hundred feet high! It contains 135 rooms, granaries, and kivas. The other two are Keet Seel (which means broken pottery) and Inscription House, named for an explorer who carved his initials and date on one of the walls. Keet Seel is the largest of the three, with 160 rooms.

One of the most surprising discoveries in Arizona was made in the San Pedro Valley. One day a rancher living there found some very large bones in a gully. He reported his find to the Arizona State Museum. A man named Emil Haury was sent to excavate the site. What he found was evidence that over eleven thousand years ago hunters had killed nine mammoths (now extinct) and had roasted some of the meat at that spot. Of course now there is nothing to see at the site. However, at the University of Arizona, there is an exhibit of the bones and the tools of the hunters exactly as the archaeologists found them in the earth.

Perhaps one of the strangest archaeological finds in the Southwest lies on the top of a high bluff along the Arizona-

California border. It was discovered in 1932 by a civilian pilot named George Palmer. While flying over the area, he looked down and, much to his surprise, saw several gigantic figures outlined in the rocky soil. One was of a man, and the others were of animals. Later, airline pilots reported still others. The curious thing about all of them is that they are so huge in outline and so shallow in depth that they can only be seen from the air! Anyone standing only a few yards away would not be able to notice them. Who made these strange effigies? What was their purpose? In 1951, a National Geographic-Smithsonian expedition went into the desert to find the answers. They finally decided that, long, long ago, Yuma Indian artists shaped the strange figures as a shrine to a legendary character called Ha-ak, a terrible monster, and its destroyer. This legend was told by an old Yuma Indian. But no one knows for *certain* who drew the effigies or why.

Though many mysteries remain in the Southwest, many facts are known. Through the scientific study of archaeological finds, we now know that hundreds of years ago—long before Europeans came to America—a great civilization existed in the Southwest United States.

Midwestern United States as it looked 16,000 years ago when the American mastodon inhabited the large expanses of spruce forest. Painted by R. G. Larson, Illinois State Museum.

Old print from Victorian book depicts a funeral feast in the Pleistocene epoch.

9

The Search for America's Past Continues

More and more archaeological sites are being discovered in the United States. In Alaska near Kotzebue, archaeologists recently unearthed ruins of ten prehistoric cultures. They found hearths, tools, and many other artifacts. Another site of interest in Alaska is in Kobuk Valley. There, in peat bogs 33,000 years old, archaeologists found fossils of woolly mammoths and evidence of hunters having killed caribou.

Not long ago in a rock shelter near Pittsburgh, Pennsylvania, archaeologists discovered fire pits and charcoal pieces showing that humans were living there fourteen to sixteen thousand years ago! This is the earliest evidence of people living in the eastern part of the United States south of Alaska.

In 1976, an early colonial settlement was discovered in Virginia. In the debris were parts of armor, a British helmet, coins, gun barrels, knives, axe heads, graves, and skeletons, and the earliest dated piece of British-American pottery ever found. From these, archaeologists are piecing together the story of life in an early colonial village.

In Missouri, some 1800 promising archaeological sites

have been identified on the Salt River. Along the Osage River, excavations have uncovered remains of mammoths and mastodons thousands of years old.

Six hundred archaeological sites are under study in the state of California. These include old Indian settlements, rock paintings, burial sites, mining camps, and Gold Rush towns—all spanning more than three thousand years of local history.

There isn't room in this book to tell about all the archaeological sites in the United States. There are thousands—from Alaska to Florida, from the shores of the Atlantic to the shores of the Pacific, and on to Hawaii. Archaeology in the United States doesn't get much publicity. Archaeologists digging in North America do not come upon great temples or tombs filled with gold artifacts.

Most of the archaeological sites in the United States are open to the public. But some are not. Archaeologists feel that some places need to be protected. Among those not open to all are Paleo (Stone Age) Indian sites. Once they have been excavated, there really is nothing to see. People of the Paleo culture left few tools or weapons in any one place because they were hunters and always on the move. Artifacts found at Paleo sites have been placed in museums.

In the early days of America there were no museums,

There are archaeological sites all over the United States. There may be one in your backyard. Here excavations in progress in 1973 at ancient site of Cherokee, Iowa, show squares in the construction area. Oldest levels at this site date back 8500 years.

historical or archaeological societies, or government agencies for protecting historical and archaeological sites. One of the first persons to take an interest in archaeology was Thomas Jefferson, the third president of the United States. In 1784, he excavated old Indian mounds to study the relics in them. Though he was not a real archaeologist, neither was he a pot hunter. He was truly interested in learning what he could about the people who had built the mounds. He kept a record and preserved the artifacts he uncovered.

The first person to do *real* archaeology in the United States was a man named Caleb Attwater. During the 1820's,

Professor Stuart Struever of Northwestern University stands beside a prehistoric crematory as he explains how the site will be excavated. It is due to the efforts of Dr. Struever that junior high school students can participate in such exciting "digs."

116

he excavated Indian mounds in the Ohio and Mississippi river valleys. It was soon after this that a number of citizens joined together and formed societies to preserve sites and ancient artifacts.

Finally, in 1906, the United States government passed laws stating that certain places of historical interest should be preserved for the public to enjoy. These places are now called national monuments or parks. Since then, many states, counties, cities, and towns have done the same. There are now many hundreds of fine archaeological museums throughout the United States. Some are located at dig sites,

but most are not. Large collections of artifacts have been gathered and placed in museums far from the sites at which they were found.

Museums are wonderful places! They tell us about our past. They preserve prehistoric remains for many to see and enjoy. Everyone cannot travel to a real archaeological site, but most people can visit a museum. There, with a little imagination, a person can picture many interesting things as they happened in the past—bison and mammoth kills, fights with the enemy on the rooftops at Mesa Verde, the building of the great walls at Pueblo Bonito, the Koster women returning home with baskets of hickory nuts, children playing with their pet dogs, and the villagers of Cahokia patiently filling baskets with earth for the construction of the great Monks Mound.

Each of us is a maker of history. As makers of history, we need to know the past—the things that have happened to make the world what it is today. Many secrets of the past are still hidden in the soil and sea. Many questions remain unanswered. In spite of all that has been learned, there is much more waiting to be discovered.

Information on Kampsville Archaeological Field Schools

How to apply for admittance to the Kampsville Archaeological Field Schools:

JUNIOR HIGH PROGRAM

Who is eligible?
Students 11–14 years of age (6th, 7th, 8th, and 9th grades) from anywhere in the United States

Site of dig
Prehistoric village in the Lower Illinois Valley

Length of session
Two weeks in summer

Applications and fees
For application and information on tuition-room-board fee write to:
    Northwestern University Archaeological Field School
    Junior High Program
    Field School Coordinator
    P. O. Box 1499
    Evanston, Illinois 60204

Field School activities
Junior high students dig by spade and trowel for artifacts, house floors, storage pits, hearths, and other evidences of human occupation; they measure and plot out their finds in the field notes; they screen the excavated dirt and later "water screen" it in the Illinois River, to retrieve minute shells, chert, charcoal, bones, and pottery; and they work in

119

their own laboratory where they wash, sort, and identify the bones, pottery, and projectile points they have unearthed. Experienced junior high students are eligible for a special lab program, spending four weeks working with a professional.

SENIOR HIGH PROGRAM

Who is eligible?
Any student from any high school in the United States who has completed sophomore year

Site of dig
Prehistoric village located in the Lower Illinois Valley

Length of session
Five weeks in summer

Applications and fees
For application and information on tuition-room-board fee write to:
  Northwestern University Archaeological Field School
  Senior High Program
  Field School Coordinator
  P. O. Box 1499
  Evanston, Illinois 60204

Field School activities
Students spend most days unearthing artifacts and the remains of buried houses and other facilities dating to more than one thousand years ago. They also have an opportunity to experiment with prehistoric technologies. Under the guidance of staff members from the Native American Studies Program, the high school students participate in projects involving the manufacture of prehistoric technology including pottery, stone tools, and wooden utensils. The students take field trips to some of the ecological zones that existed in the Lower Illinois Valley during prehistoric times and still remain today. In each of these zones they are briefed on the specific resources that prehistoric people took from there.

ADULT PROGRAMS

The following adult level programs are offered at the Kampsville Archaeological Center:

Field School for University Students (Undergraduate and Graduate)
Adult Field School* and Laboratory Program
Native American Studies
Teachers Workshop

*ADULTS OF ALL AGES, WITH OR WITHOUT PREVIOUS BACKGROUND IN ARCHAEOLOGY, ARE ELIGIBLE.

For information and fees on the adult programs write to:
Northwestern University Archaeology
Field School Coordinator
P. O. Box 1499
Evanston, Illinois 60204

Index

Alaska, 16, 42, 47, 113
Amateur helpers, 41–43, 45–48
Amerindians, definition of, 80
Animals
  domesticated, 82
  extinct types of, 16, 41, 42, 46, 47, 108, 110, 113
  as food source, 82, 84
  lions of carved stone, New Mexico, 108
  remains examined in lab, 68, 70
Anthropology, definition of, 35. *See also* 40, 56
Archaeological dating, *see* Dating techniques
Archaeologists, definition of, 13
  amateur and volunteer, 41–43, 45–48
  first in U.S., 116
  underwater, 28
Archaeology, definition of, 13
  amateurs in, 41–43, 45–48
  classical or old, 34–36
  fakes and forgers in, 45
  a fun science, 41
  how things get buried, 14–20
  how to dig, 60–61, 63–66

Archaeology *(Continued)*
  how to preserve finds, 45
  modern or new, 34–38, 40
  robbers in, 20, 45
  salvage, 30, 53
  as a science, 40
  techniques used in, 32–34, 37
  tools used in, 63
  underwater, 28
  in U.S., 29–30, 46–47, 113, 115–118
  where to dig, 23, 25–26, 28–29
Arizona, *see* Sites
Artifacts, definition of, 18
  amateurs and, 43, 77
  ancient tombs and, 31
  children and, 41–42
  at Cliff Palace, 103
  colonial, 113
  new archaeology and, 36
  Paleo, 115
  at Pueblo Bonito, 107
  underwater, 28
  where to look for, 23, 25–26
Asia Minor, 26–28
Attwater, Caleb, 116–117

123

Babylonia, 31
Balcony House, 103
Bandelier, Adolf, 108
Betatakin, 110
Black Hills, 46
Bronze Age, 32
Burial practices
  at Cahokia, 92–93
  cemetery, 6000-year-old, 47
  dog burial, 82
  at Koster site, 82

Cahokia, 89–93, 96, 118
  agriculture, 98
  arts and crafts, 96
  Monks Mound, 91–92
  "Woodhenge," 93, 96
Carbon 14, *see* Dating techniques
Caves, 25, 38
  canyons, 99, 100, 108, 110
  paintings in, 108
  pit caves, 25
Cedar Tree House, 103
Chaco Canyon, 105, 107–108
Cherokee, 96
Chert, definition of, 55
Classical archaeology, 34–36
Cliff dwellers, 99–101, 103, 105,
    107–108, 110–111
  agriculture, 100
  houses, 99
  kivas, 100
  pottery and art, 100, 107
  tools, 100
Cliff Palace, 101, 103
Clovis site, 110
Constantine the Great, 31
Copán, Honduras, 26

Cultures, definition of, 20
  Egyptian, 34
  Greek, 34
  Jersey Bluff, 77–78
  Mississippian, 90
  North American prehistoric, 34,
    37, 87, 96, 113
  Paleo, 115
  Roman, 34

Data, definition of, 56
Dating techniques
  Bronze Age, 32
  Carbon 14, 34
  Iron Age, 32
  radiocarbon, 34, 35
  Stone Age, 32
  tree-ring, 33
Datum post, definition of, 56
Debris, definition of, 56
Dinosaur Canyon, 110
Douglass, Andrew, 33

Earthquakes, 15
Effigy, definition of, 89
  Fig Island Shell Ring, 89
  Rock Eagle Effigy, 89
  Serpent Mound, 89
  in Wisconsin, 89
  Yuma Indian, 111
Egypt, 17–18, 34, 41, 46, 47, 80,
  90
Egyptian hieroglyphics, 31
Egyptians, 96

Fauna, definition of, 56
Fig Island Shell Ring, 89
Flotation, definition of, 66

Folsom site, 41, 108
Forms, archaeological, 56
Fossil, definition of, 16. *See also* 25, 30, 113
Foundation for Illinois Archaeology, 50
Frijoles Canyon, 108

Glaciers, 15
Goosefoot, 38
Granite, 25
Greece, 34

Ha-ak monster, 111
Haury, Emil, 110
Helton, Harlan, 77
Horizons, definition of, 20
  in Asia Minor, 27
  at Koster, 79, 82, 84

Ice Age, 41
Inscription House, 110
Iron Age, 32

Jefferson, Thomas, 116
Judd, Neil, 105

Kampsville, 48, 49–51, 53, 55–61, 63–66, 68, 70–72, 74–76
  adult program, 51, 53
  junior high program, 48, 50, 53, 55–61, 63–66, 68, 70–72, 74–76
  research and teaching center, 50, 51, 53, 68
  senior high program, *see* junior high program
Keet Seel, 110

Kivas, 100, 101, 103
Knotwood, 38
Kobuk Valley, 113
Koster, 77–80, 82, 84–85, 87, 118
  animals at, 82, 84
  burials at, 82
  food at, 82, 84
  houses at, 80, 82
  how discovered, 77
  how named, 79
  importance of, 79–80
  plants at, 84
  trade, 84
  warfare, 84
Koster, Mary, 79
Koster, Theodore, 77, 79
Kotzebue, 113

Lava, definition of, 16
Libby, Willard, 34
Limestone, 25
Line level, 57
Lithics, definition of, 57
Long House, 103

MacDougal, Genevieve, 48
Magnetometer, 29
Mammoth, 42, 46, 47, 110, 115, 118
Marble, 15
Marshelder, 38
Mayan ruins, 26
Mesa Verde, 103, 105, 118
Metal detector, 25–26
Midden, definition of, 57
Monks Mound, 90–91, 98, 118
Mound builders, 89–93, 96–98. *See also* Effigy *and* Mounds

Mounds, 23, 27, 42, 43, 116, 117
  Cahokia, 89–93, 96, 118
  Fig Island Shell Ring, 89
  Monks Mound, 90–91, 98, 118
  in Ohio, 89
  Rock Eagle Effigy, 89
  Serpent Mound, 89
  in Wisconsin, 89

National Geographic Society, 33,
  105, 111
New archaeology, 34–38, 40
Northwestern University, 48, 50,
  77, 78

Obsidian, definition of, 84

Paleo Indian sites, 115
Palmer, George, 111
Peat bogs, 17, 25
Plants
  botany lab, 70
  prehistoric, 16, 37, 38, 80, 84
Pollen analysis, 37, 70, 98
Pompeii, 31, 41
"Pot hunter," 45, 116
Pottery, 37, 42, 55, 58, 72, 77, 84,
  96, 100, 107, 113
Pueblo Bonito, 105, 107–108, 118

Radiocarbon dating, see Dating
  techniques
Rock, 15, 25
  tarp, 58
Rock Eagle Effigy, 89
Rock shelter, 25, 103, 113
Rome, 34
Rosetta Stone, 31, 41

Salvage archaeology, 30, 53
San Pedro Valley, 110
Schliemann, Heinrich, 26–28,
  31
Serpent Mound, 89
Sherd, definition of, 57
Siberia, 16–17, 42
Silt, 15–17
Siltstone, 25
Site, definition of, 57
  safety at, 60
Sites, archaeological, in United
  States
  Alaska, 113
  Arizona, 41, 99, 110, 111
  California, 115
  Colorado, 41, 99, 100–105, 118
  Connecticut, 46, 47
  Florida, 47
  Georgia, 89
  Illinois, 39, 41, 46, 47, 49, 50,
    77–80, 82, 84–85, 87, 89–93,
    96–98
  Maine, 47
  Mississippi, 117
  Missouri, 113, 115
  New Mexico, 41, 99, 105–108,
    109, 110
  Ohio, 89, 117
  Oklahoma, 42–43
  Pennsylvania, 47, 113
  South Carolina, 89
  South Dakota, 46
  Virginia, 47, 113
  Wisconsin, 89
Smithsonian Institution, 33, 105,
  111

Soil
 analysis, 37
 color of, 65
 preserving qualities, 17, 19
 sterile, 57
Sonar-scanning, 28–29
Square, definition of, 57. *See also*
  60–61, 99–101, 103, 105, 107–
  108, 110–111
Stone Age, 32, 46–47
Stonehenge, 46, 47, 80, 93
Strata, 15–16
Struever, Dr. Stuart, 48, 77, 85
Sun Temple, 103

Tarp, definition of, 57
 tarping squares, 71
Temper, definition of, 58
Thomsen, Christian, 32
Tools, ancient, 16–17, 32, 42

Tree-ring dating, *see* Dating
 techniques
Troy, 26–28, 31
Tutankhamon, 33–34

Underwater archaeology, 28
University of Arizona, 110
University of Chicago, 35

Valley of the Kings, 17–18
Volcano, 16

Woodhenge, 93, 96

Yucatan, 46
Yuma Indian effigies, 110–111

Zooarchaeology, definition of,
 74
 osteology lab, 70

About the Author

As a child, Velma Ford Morrison had a reputation among her family and friends for curiosity about plants, animals, and people. Her early years were spent working in her experimental garden; raising rabbits, bees, and unusual breeds of poultry; and exploring the woods, fields, and streams in search of specimens for her many collections. One of the highlights of her childhood was a trip she made with her family to visit the Bad Lands of South Dakota. It was there she found her first *real* Indian artifacts—a broken arrow point and a stone axe head. Nothing could have excited her more. From then on her interest in archaeology and anthroplogy grew by leaps and bounds. She began reading and studying everything she could find on these and related subjects. Her studies focused not only on the cultural remains of ancient populations but also on heredity and other aspects of ancient human biology.

Few people have traveled more widely to study human history. To date the author's journeys have taken her to Mexico, South and Central America, the Orient, Thailand, Nepal, India, Iran, Africa (North, South, and East), Australia (including the Outback), New Zealand, New Guinea, the South Pacific Islands, the Galapagos, the U.S.S.R. from West Russia to Siberia, Europe, and every state in the United States including Alaska and Hawaii. She is presently planning a trip to China. When asked, "Of all the different cultures of the world that you have studied, which have you found to be the most interesting?" she replied, "Those of our own Native Americans—the American Indians."

Mrs. Morrison's background includes teaching as well as research and writing. She has had sixteen books published. With her husband, Hugh, she lives in Princeton, Illinois, when they are not traveling. The Morrisons have four children.

930.1   Morrison, Velma Ford
M83   Going on a dig

FEB 10 1984	DATE DUE		
FEB 21 1984			
FEB 27 1984			
FEB 29 1984			
MAR 14 1984			
MAR 29 1984			
APR 4 1984			
MAX 21 1985			